Upper Cape Cod

oversize
917.44

First published in the United States of America by
PilotPress Publishers, Inc., James R. Franklin, Publisher
110 Westchester Road
Newton, Massachusetts 02458
Telephone: (617) 332-0703
www.PilotPress.com
and
Twin Light Publishers, Inc., Doris R. Patey, Publisher
Ten Hale Street
Rockport, Massachusetts 01966
Telephone: (978) 546-7398

Aerial photography courtesy of
Rockport Publishers, Inc.

ISBN 0-9677537-0-8

10 9 8 7 6 5 4 3 2 1

Designer: Leeann Leftwich
        Email: clldesign@aol.com

Cover image: Babs Armour

Printed in China

Upper Cape Cod

A PHOTOGRAPHIC PORTRAIT

PILOTPRESS PUBLISHERS • TWIN LIGHTS PUBLISHERS

ROBERT YOUNG

Star-Spangled Banner

The Bourne Bridge over the Cape Cod Canal, with the old railroad bridge in the background. The federal government built the Bourne and Sagamore Bridges, the two gateways to Cape Cod, in 1933 during the Great Depression. They are still maintained by the United States Army Corps of Engineers. The flag in the photograph flies from the stern of a tour boat.

FOREWORD

PilotPress Publishers is pleased to bring you this photographic portrait.

The book presents many quality photographs of the Upper Cape that are the work of amateur, semi-professional and professional photographers who submitted their work as part of a photographic contest.

These photographs are representative of the area. We ask that you view them with the same enthusiasm and excitement experienced by the photographers who live in or who visited the area and were prompted to record their memories on film.

We would like to congratulate all whose work was selected for the book and, in particular, we would like to highlight the following photographers:

FIRST PRIZE
Nobska Light, Woods Hole
Babs Armour
New York, New York

Nobska Lighthouse, on Nobska Point in Woods Hole, Falmouth. The original Nobska Light was built in 1828; in 1878 the government replaced the old wooden tower with the steel lighthouse that stands today.

Babs Armour's photographs have been included in numerous group shows, exhibited in galleries throughout the Northeast and California, and were featured in a solo show in New York City in 1993. Her work, which is in both private and corporate collections, has won many awards and has been featured on WCBS-TV in New York and on ABC's Good Morning America. Ms. Armour has been photographing Cape Cod for the past twelve years. Having grown up in New England, she has a special love for the area, and, as a photographer, a particular affinity for the light, variety and beauty of the Upper Cape. When on the Cape, her camera is never very far from her side.

SECOND PRIZE
Harvest Time
Sallyann Murphy
Mashpee, MA

Gathering cranberries, Mashpee. The cranberry is a Cape Cod tradition. The Wampanoags spiced their venison with cranberries and instructed the white settlers in the red berries' many uses. In 1677 settlers shipped ten barrels of cranberries to King Charles II, offering His Majesty a taste of the New World. Commercial cultivation of cranberries on the Cape set a record in 1895, when 150,000 barrels were harvested, worth one million dollars.

Sallyann Murphy retired from teaching in the Worcester, Massachusetts's public schools in 1992 to pursue her dream of living on Cape Cod. She describes it as a "now or never decision" since her three children were all married with families of their own. She has never regretted the opportunity of this new adventure as she has found it a rewarding, fulfilling and learning experience. She now explores every pond, marsh and ocean shore. Her camera allows her to share with her family and friends the stories of life that she finds.

THIRD PRIZE
Primary Colors
David Gouveia

All is quiet on an early summer's morning at West Falmouth Harbor.

David F. Gouveia is a surgeon at Morton Hospital in Taunton, Massachusetts. Photography has been a lifetime hobby. He has received several prizes in photography both locally and nationally. One of his photographs, "Bermuda Rooftops" is in the permanent collection of the Fuller Art Museum in Brockton, Massachusetts. The parents of four children, he and his wife divide their time between homes in Taunton and West Falmouth, Massachusetts.

MASSACHUSETTS

CAPE COD CANAL

SAGAMORE

6

SANDWICH

6A

MONUMENT BEACH

28

136

BOURNE

POCASSET

CATAUMET

MASHPEE

151

WEST FALMOUTH

COTUIT

FALMOUTH

WAQUOIT

EAST FALMOUTH

WOODS HOLE

INTRODUCTION

It is called the Upper Cape, against all logic and cartographic evidence. Look at a map: the Upper Cape juts south between Buzzards Bay and Nantucket Sound, while the Lower Cape, far to the east, bends like an elbow and rises due north to the balled fist of Provincetown. On the map, the Upper Cape is lower. No one has ever been able to tell me how these backward-seeming designations were arrived at, but there they are, and Cape Codders are comfortable with them.

Of the four towns of the Upper Cape, Sandwich, the northernmost, is the oldest. It was incorporated in 1639, two years after Edmund Freeman received permission from the governor of the Plymouth Colony to establish a settlement whose purpose was "to worship God and make money." The town today has an antique feel. Its clapboard and weathered-shingle buildings, its mill pond and towering trees, comprise a kind of living museum, and there is the ancient whisper of the wind in the great marsh by Cape Cod Bay.

To the south lies Bourne, which was part of Sandwich until 1884. The town is squeezed between the vast woods of the Camp Edwards Military Reservation and the waters of the Cape Cod Canal and Buzzards Bay. Its shoreline is a jigsaw puzzle of inlets, natural harbors, bights, necks, and miniature islands. During his presidency, Grover Cleveland summered in Bourne, in a mansion called Gray Gables, above the warm and tranquil Bay, where the sunsets defy description, as you will see.

Falmouth sprawls across the southwest corner of the Cape. Religious dissenters from Barnstable and Sandwich, led by Isaac Robinson, a Congregationalist, and Jonathan Hatch, a Quaker, settled it in 1660. It is the second largest town on the Cape and growing fast, but Falmouth's scattered villages have proven stubbornly immune to change.

And then there is Mashpee, the ancestral home of the Mashpee Wampanoags, abutting Falmouth on the northwest. Development has taken a toll on the primeval Mashpee woods, and newcomers and Native Americans have often been at odds as a result. In 1995, the Mashpee National Wildlife Refuge was created, a treasure of 5,871 acres, and enmities cooled. Today, the town retains a rural flavor, and tribal traditions run strong.

This book gets you close to the sea and soil, the landmarks and architecture, of the Upper Cape. There's stability here, something enduring and timeless, for all the changes the modern age has brought. The sun sets over Buzzards Bay just as the first settlers saw it, and the Village Green of Falmouth slumbers undisturbed down the centuries. *The Upper Cape: A Photographic Portrait* is about permanence, the undying essence of a place called Cape Cod. It is about towns that predate the Revolution, and sights our ancestors saw. The Cape, really, is still a lovely piece of America.

THE VILLAGES OF FALMOUTH

BRENDA SWITHENBANK

Cascade

This wheelbarrow from
another century is put to
aesthetic use in a private
garden in Falmouth.
Well-groomed yards and
gardens are a visual pleasure
throughout the Upper Cape.

OPPOSITE

GINNY MESSMORE

Home Port

Cataumet Harbor, North
Falmouth. As its waterfront
suggests, Cataumet is an
affluent and tidy village of
considerable visual beauty.

JOHN D. WILLIAMS

Slack Tide

West Falmouth Harbor.

GAYLE HEASLIP

Midas Touch

Snug Harbor, West Falmouth.
This quiet backwater is tucked
inside the north corner of West
Falmouth Harbor and is true to
its name.

JOHN D. WILLIAMS

Taxis

Dinghies at West Falmouth Harbor.

MARIE CORRIVEAU

Fire in the Sky

West Falmouth Harbor at sundown.

RITA L. WILLIAMS

Still Water

This boathouse at West
Falmouth, weather-beaten and
handsome, is a familiar sight in
that tranquil village on
Buzzards Bay.

TOP

JOHN D. WILLIAMS

Redoubt

Beach grass can hold a dune together and prevent coastal erosion. Like the dunes themselves, it is fragile and vulnerable to human intrusion. Old Silver Beach, North Falmouth.

ABOVE

DAVID GOUVEIA

Mother-of-Pearl

Nightfall at Old Silver Beach in North Falmouth.

FOLLOWING PAGE

KAREN RINALDO

Parfait

Chapoquoit Island, West Falmouth. The island was originally called Hog Island, because farmers kept their pigs there, giving them run of the place. It was renamed at the turn of the century, when it was settled as a summer colony. The fashionable newcomers, evidently, thought "Hog Island" lacked appropriate elegance and melody. Today, entrants in the fall Beetle Cat races in West Falmouth Harbor style themselves the Hog Island Racers, keeping the homely old name alive.

21

KAREN RINALDO

Band of Gold

A dance at twilight in the still-water of Buzzards Bay, Old Silver Beach, North Falmouth.

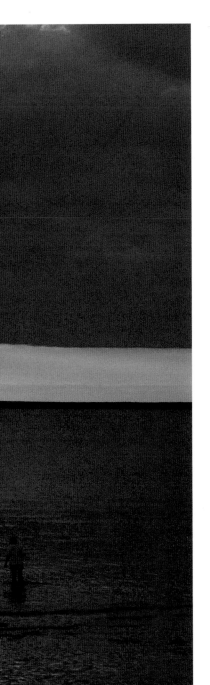

DAVID GOUVEIA

A Day at the Beach

Old Silver Beach, North Falmouth. Old Silver, broad and sugar- white, cradling the warm and quiet waters of Buzzards Bay, is one of Cape Cod's most popular beaches.

JOHN D. WILLIAMS

Cutting Edge

Wind surfer on Nantucket Sound.

OPPOSITE

HEIDI BRATTON

Conclave

Sundown at Old Silver
Beach, North Falmouth.

ABOVE

DAVID GOUVEIA

Heaven's Gate

Evening at West
Falmouth Harbor.

JOHN D. WILLIAMS

Silence

Reflections in early morning in West Falmouth.

JOHN D. WILLIAMS

Burgoo

An offshore fog at Old Silver Beach in North Falmouth. Cape fogs, especially in the summertime, are a frequent feature of the landscape.

HEIDI BRATTON

Sumner Morn

Wing Road Farm House, North Falmouth.

MARIE CORRIVEAU

Sea Breeze

West Falmouth Harbor on a not-quite-still day. In the first half of the 19th century, a salt works on the harbor shore comprised the village's major industry. Today, the harbor is an abundant source of shellfish and a popular sailing ground.

MARYLYNNE GABEL

Body Language

Navigating the inlets at Chapoquoit Beach in West Falmouth.

MARIE CORRIVEAU

Angles

A Sunfish at West Falmouth Harbor. This petite sailboat may be the most utilized single design in all of sailing. It can be manned by one or two persons and is the perfect craft for beginners. The colorful and speedy little boats are an emblem of summer on the Cape and Islands.

HEIDI BRATTON

Spires

Fortress and towers on Chapoquoit Beach in West Falmouth.

CECILIA WORTH

Sentinals

Old Field Cove from Fassett's Point, West Falmouth.

TOP

CECILIA WORTH

Pastel

Sloat's Dock on Old Field Cove, West Falmouth.

ABOVE

DAVID GOUVEIA

B & B

The Chapoquoit Inn, in the historic district of West Falmouth, one of many old houses that have been turned into bed and break-fasts.

CECILIA WORTH
Deep Freeze
Ice on Black Beach in West
Falmouth.

JOEL PETERSON

Outpost

Winter in West Falmouth.

JOEL PETERSON

Bottoms Up

Cape winters are sometimes bitter, more often mild. Snow on the mainland may fall as rain on the Cape, warmed by the gentle air of the Gulf Stream. In the dead of winter, five to ten degrees warmer than Boston is the rule.

JOEL PETERSON
Snowbound
Ice on Vineyard Sound.
Everyone who has lived for a
while on Buzzards Bay or
Vineyard Sound can remember
those bodies of water freezing
up, but it's a rare occurrence in
the usually wet and changeable
Cape winters.

FOLLOWING PAGE

JUDY SINGER
Plumage

Jenkins Pond in Falmouth. Captain Weston Jenkins was commander
of the Falmouth Artillery Company during the War of 1812. In
January 1814, Captain Jenkins refused a British demand that he
surrender his field pieces, whereupon the British brig Nimrod
bombarded the town for several hours, inflicting little damage but
writing vivid memories in town lore. Later that year, Captain Jenkins
and 30 volunteers captured the British privateer Retaliation in a
surprise nocturnal raid at Tarpaulin Cove. The British surrendered
without firing a shot.

HEIDI BRATTON

Summer Bounty

Enjoying the strawberries at the Tony Andrews Farm in East Falmouth. In the first half of the 20th century, Falmouth strawberries were a renowned New England delicacy; in 1930, 2,300,000 quarts of berries were shipped to the Boston market. The Andrews Farm has been in the family since 1925. It is one of two working farms that survive in Falmouth.

JOEL PETERSON

Afternoon Light

The Waquoit Congregational Church was built in 1848. Eighteen whaling captains are buried in its cemetery.

GREAT POND EAST FALMOUTH

GREEN POND EAST FALMOUTH

WAQUOIT

COREN MILBURY

Teeth

Pilings at Maravista Beach, East Falmouth. Maravista means, "sea view", and from its south-facing shore the ocean panorama is limitless, with Martha's Vineyard, a mere bump, away to the west.

AMY KRANZ

Roundel

These old timbers, bleached by sun and sea salt, have been here awhile. A forgotten storm deposited them high up on Menauhant Beach in East Falmouth.

TARA NYE

Mirror Image

Night falls over Waquoit Bay in Falmouth. The Waquoit Bay National Estuarine Research Reserve comprises several thousand wild acres. The federal government moved to preserve it at the prodding of the Mashpee Wampanoags.

GINNY MESSMORE

Winter Blanket

Menauhant Beach, East Falmouth, under a carpet of new snow and a western sky washed in the light of the setting sun.

COREN MILBURY

Waiting

Old skiffs, scarred but serviceable, await the next launch on Great River, off Waquoit Bay in Falmouth.

GINNY MESSMORE

Study in Blue and Gold

Bourne's Pond in East Falmouth. In 1638, Richard Bourne of Sandwich helped the Wampanoag chief Quachatisset register a deed to the Mashpee tribal lands with the Plymouth Colony. The General Court ratified the grant in 1682.

ABOVE

KAREN RINALDO

Old Glory

The Falmouth Village Green was laid out in 1749. Here, the Falmouth Militia drilled as the American colonies drifted toward revolution. Some of the town's oldest houses are gathered around the triangular lawn of the Green.

OPPOSITE

MARYLYNNE GABEL

Cotton Candy

Katherine Lee Bates Road, Falmouth. Bates was born in Falmouth in 1859. She wrote 13 books and achieved immortality with a single poem, "America, the Beautiful." Her house near the Village Green is a museum owned by the Falmouth Historical Society.

MARTHA COX

Informal Gathering

Falmouth Harbor with St. Thomas
Chapel in the background. The
harbor was landlocked originally
and known as Deacon's Pond. The
opening to Nantucket Sound was
cut in 1907. General George
Goethals, who built the Panama
Canal, acted as an engineering
advisor to the project.

EILEEN O'CONNELL

Home Before Dark

A garden gate on Gifford Street,
Falmouth, in the dying light of a
spring evening.

OPPOSITE

COREN MILBURY

Fireball

The sun goes down over Little Pond in Falmouth. Little Pond is the smallest of the long-fingered inlets that penetrate Falmouth's south shore on Vineyard and Nantucket Sounds. The town's first inhabitants settled along Little Pond in 1661.

ABOVE

JUDY SINGER

Easy Rider

A swan on Salt Pond, Falmouth. Tradition holds that swans are never found on salt or brackish water, but the axiom is amply disproved on Cape Cod.

RIGHT

MARYLYNNE GABEL

Ramparts

Menauhant Beach in East Falmouth. Menauhant was Falmouth's first real summer colony. It was a fashionable settlement, built mostly along the shore, where you can look out over Nantucket Sound to the bending rim of the horizon.

COREN MILBURY

Solitude

Twilight at Racing Beach, Falmouth.
In the spring and fall the striped bass
and bluefish move into shallow waters
off Cape Cod. Look for them in April,
and again in mid-September. The Cape
has been a fisherman's paradise since
colonial times.

COREN MILBURY

Aura

Sunset at Racing Beach,
Falmouth. This wide barrier
beach stretches itself on
Buzzards Bay between
Gunning Point and the Knob.
Its name goes back to the 19th
century, when horse races
were held here.

MICHAEL PETRIZZO

Blue on Blue

Falmouth Harbor, inbound
view. The harbor is usually
referred to as Falmouth Inner
Harbor, a designation that has
survived since the harbor was
opened in 1907. Then, the
original harbor area was the
outer harbor, and the newer,
deeper reach the inner harbor.

JOEL PETERSON

Awakening

Day lilies and lobster buoys above Salt Pond in Falmouth. The lilies bloom in mid-June, eastward-leaning on their long stems, opening trumpet-like to the morning light and closing tight when darkness falls.

JOEL PETERSON

Sailors' Delight

Sunset over Salt Pond in Falmouth

KAREN RINALDO

Shadows

The Congregational Church by
the Falmouth Village Green.
The steeple bell was cast by
Paul Revere and bears this
inscription: "The living to the
church I call, and to the grave I
summon all."

GINNY MESSMORE

Wind Damage

A wind fence staggers in the
aftermath of a hard blow at
Menauhant Beach, East
Falmouth. The winter winds can
break down and reconfigure the
fragile beaches; the wind fences
help hold the shifting sands.

COREN MILBURY

Feathers

Winter marsh grass at Salt Pond,
Falmouth, at sunset. The salt
marsh is one of the richest habi-
tats of the Western Hemisphere
— a lush garden of grasses and
other fresh water plants that
have adapted to the salinity of
the marsh, and the residence of
myriad forms of wildlife, including microbes, fish, birds and
rodents.

WOODS HOLE

QUISSETT

LAURA BURRITT

First Bloom

Spohr's Garden, Woods Hole,
Falmouth. These three splendid
acres are privately owned but
open to the public. From spring to
fall, something is always in bloom.

OPPOSITE

ANN AUKAMP

Rock of Ages

The Church of the Messiah in
Woods Hole, Falmouth, was built
in 1888. Both the church and the
land it stands on were gifts of
Joseph Story Fay, a wealthy
Boston merchant and Woods
Hole's first summer resident.

Carolyn B. Corcoran
Airborne

"The Airplane House" on Juniper Point, Woods Hole, Falmouth. It was nicknamed by neighbors for its grace and aerodynamic appearance. The house was built in about 1912 as a summer home for Charles W. Crane, United States minister to China in 1920 and 1921. The architects were William Gray Purcell and George Grant Elmslie, who worked in Chicago for Louis Sullivan, a pioneer modernist who schooled Frank Lloyd Wright.

ABOVE

ABOVE

KRISTIN PETERSON

Breakers

High Wind at Nobska Point,
Woods Hole, Falmouth.

OPPOSITE

DAVID GOUVEIA

Souvenirs

Mooring buoys bedeck an exte-
rior wall of the Landfall
Restaurant in Woods Hole,
Falmouth.

FOLLOWING PAGE

BABS ARMOUR

Pickets

At Nobska Lighthouse, Woods
Hole, Falmouth.

JOEL PETERSON

Backwater

The Eel Pond in Woods Hole,
Falmouth, snuggles safely behind the
village itself, connected to Vineyard
Sound by a narrow inlet that passes
under a drawbridge. Pedestrians on
Water Street like to loiter on the bridge
and call out to the boats as they slip
past below.

JOEL PETERSON

Veil

Little Harbor, Woods Hole,
Falmouth.

JOEL PETERSON

Godspeed

Shenandoah, a 108-foot square
topsail schooner owned by
Robert Douglas of Martha's
Vineyard, is a familiar sight on
Vineyard Sound in the summer-
time. She sails out of Vineyard
Haven on leisurely weeklong
cruises. Reservations required.

JOEL PETERSON

Wind Song

Nobska Point, Woods Hole, from the west. Nobska is the southernmost point of Cape Cod. The view here is what passengers on the Martha's Vineyard ferries see as the boats move in and out of Woods Hole Harbor.

MARIE CORRIVEAU

Mariners' Friend

Nobska Lighthouse on a clear, crisp day.

ABOVE

JOEL PETERSON

Ornament

Skiff in Quissett Harbor,
Falmouth.

OPPOSITE

DANIEL GORMAN

Indigo

August Dawn at Quissett
Harbor, Falmouth.

HEIDI BRATTON

Sketches in the Sand

On Woodneck Beach in
Woods Hole, Falmouth.

JOEL PETERSON

Beaten Path

Dunes and beach grass,
Falmouth. Where people walk,
the beach grass vanishes. So
does much wildlife, especially
the tiny, dovelike piping plover,
which nests on Cape beaches
from late March to August.
The U.S. Fish and Wildlife
Service and the Massachusetts
Audubon Society, among other
environmental organizations,
have adopted management pro-
grams for the piping plover.

JOEL PETERSON

Summer Crowd

Woods Hole and the Eel Pond.
There's something both cozy
and bohemian about Woods
Hole in the summertime. Water
Street and its homey little
shops and restaurants are aboil
with people of all descriptions
— locals, tourists, fishermen,
marine biologists from the
Oceanographic Institute and
Marine Biological Laboratory.
Dress is informal, and life
moves at a leisurely pace.

JOEL PETERSON

Clearing Sky

The Buzzards Bay shore of
Woods Hole, Falmouth.

CAROLYN B. CORCORAN

Firelight

Sippewissett, Falmouth: The sun goes down over Buzzards Bay. The Buzzards Bay sunsets are one of the Upper Cape's treasured natural resources.

ABOVE

JOEL PETERSON

Artist at Work

Karen Rinaldo on the Knob at Quissett, Falmouth. The Knob juts into Buzzards Bay by Quissett Harbor, a 13-acre tract of unspoiled field and scrub. It is open to the public.

RIGHT

KAREN RINALDO

"The Knob"

Watercolor by Karen Rinaldo. Ms. Rinaldo is a Falmouth resident whose studio is found at the entrance to Falmouth Harbor.

JOEL PETERSON

Leg Work

The Falmouth Road Race, held
on the third Sunday of August,
draws the best distance runners
in the world, as well as thou-
sands of recreational joggers.
The 7.1 mile course follows the
shore line from Woods Hole to
Falmouth Heights.

JOEL PETERSON

Woods Hole Sunset

Early September sun sets over
Woods Hole Oceangraphic
Institute and Sea Education
Association vessels in Woods
Hole harbor.

JOEL PETERSON

Filaments

The delicacy of beach grass is vividly suggested in this close-up study. Shallow-rooted and vulnerable, the beach grasses are the threads that hold most beaches together.

JOEL PETERSON

Blue Mirror

Little Harbor, Woods Hole, Falmouth. This almost perfect rectangle of a harbor is your first view of Woods Hole as you come in on the main road, as almost all first-time visitors do. The harbor, though open to Vineyard Sound, is quiet in all weathers, as picturesque and undisturbed by time as Woods Hole itself. On the west side of the harbor the United States Coast Guard base huddles inconspicuously.

JOEL PETERSON

Summer Weekend

A nearly full house at Quissett
Harbor, Falmouth.

CAPE COD CANAL

CATAUMET

BABS ARMOUR

On the Beach

The Spit, Popponessett, Falmouth. This barrier spit, which separates Popponessett Bay from Nantucket Sound, once extended to the Cotuit shore, locking in what is now the Bay. It was breached by the 1938 hurricane.

JENNIFER WALTERREIT

Room With A View

A window to the Wings Neck Land Trust, Pocasset. Wings Neck is a crooked two-mile salient into Buzzards Bay covered with upland woods and marshland. The trust was created by residents; the open land remains private, but restricted from development.

GINNY MESSMORE

Follow the Leader

A family of swans on Shawme Pond, Sandwich. The demure-appearing mother swan is a fierce protector of her young, as many a dog has learned to its chagrin.

NAN CHUTE

Family Outing

On Shawme Pond, Sandwich. Shawme Pond, originally Shawme Lake, is an integral part of historic Sandwich. The old town hall, the Hoxie House, the Thornton Burgess House and the Dexter Grist Mill all sit along its banks. Ducks, swans, pond lilies and willows all thrive on Shawme, a feast of delights best accessible by canoe.

SALLYANN MURPHY

Patriarch

Early Morning at the Dexter Grist Mill on Shawme Pond, Sandwich. Thomas Dexter, one of the town's founders, built the mill in about 1640. It was restored in 1961; today, the public is welcome to watch its grindstone and wooden gears in action, and to take home a bag of ground corn.

ABOVE

SALLYANN MURPHY

Under Her Wing

Swan and cygnets on Shawme Pond in Sandwich. Swans are ubiquitous on Cape Cod, as they are across most of the continental United States. The elegant bird subsists almost entirely on aquatic vegetation and is one of the rare species that mate for life.

OPPOSITE

VIVIAN FRINK

Wilderness

The Pocasset River marshes from Shore Road, Bourne. The Pocasset River is a designated area of critical environmental concern. Numerous endangered species still flourish here, including musk, spotted, and box turtles.

Layer Cake

Replica of a Shaker barn, Heritage Plantation, Sandwich. The barn
contains the antique automobile collection.

Carousel

This carousel at the Heritage Plantation museum in Sandwich was built in 1912 and is still whirling young riders round and round. The Heritage Plantation occupies 76 acres threaded with walking paths and magnificently adorned with flowering shrubs. Its buildings contain an eclectic mix of exhibits, including artifacts, old weapons, antique cars, and early American paintings.

Courtesy Heritage Plantation

Duesy

Gary Cooper's 1931 Duesenberg in the Shaker Barn at the Heritage Plantation, Sandwich.

Courtesy Heritage Plantation

DAVID GOUVEIA

Royalty

The Mashpee Wampanoag Powwow: the Princess Contest.

DAVID GOUVEIA

Regalia

The Mashpee Wampanoag Powwow is held every Fourth of July weekend. The powwow, or tribal reunion, is a universal tradition among Native Americans. Tribes from Canada and across the northeast United States attend the Mashpee powwow, which features ancient ceremonial dances and the crowning of a princess. Spectators are welcome.

SALLYANN MURPHY

Stalker

The great blue heron is the largest and most common of the Cape's coastal herons, with a wingspan of some 70 inches. It subsists on fish, crustaceans, and amphibians—a patient hunter that can remain perfectly still as the minutes crawl by, waiting for its prey to wander within range of its lethal bill.

COREN MILBURY

All in a Row

Popponessett Island, Mashpee.

LEFT

SALLYANN MURPHY

Hard Right

The boardwalk across the great marsh in Sandwich. In 1991, Hurricane Bob destroyed the original boardwalk, built in 1874.

OPPOSITE

CATHLEEN BRODERICK

A Distant Shore

The Cape Cod Canal, from the Bourne side. The Canal was a century-old dream when digging finally began in June 1909, under the aegis of New York financier August Belmont. It took five years to finish the job, a roughly ten-mile waterway between Cape Cod Bay and Buzzards Bay. The Canal saves coastal traffic 150 miles of travel and passage of the dangerous shoals off the outer Cape. It was privately operated for fourteen years, and then purchased by the United States government in 1928.

JUDY SINGER

Beckoning

Bridge to South Cape Beach, Popponessett, Mashpee.

HEIDI BRATTON

Flier

At the Barnstable County Fair in East Falmouth. The July event runs for six days and features livestock and produce competition, live music, rides, and plenty of food.

CUTTYHUNK ISLAND

HADLEY'S HARBOR

JOEL PETERSON

Weather Eye

Watson cruising Vineyard Sound.

JOEL PETERSON

Respite

Lobster Pots at Hadley's Harbor, Naushon

JOEL PETERSON

Triple Play

Hereshoffs at Hadley's Harbor, Naushon. The famous hull, with its deep keel and extraordinary stability, was designed in 1914 by Nathaniel Greene Hereshoff of Bristol, Rhode Island. "The Wizard of Bristol" had been asked by friends to create a small, steady boat in which their children could safely learn to sail.

PRISCILLA ELLIS

Sun Bathers

Harbor seals off Naushon.
These playful mammals, also
called common seals, inhabit
the coastal waters of the Cape
and Islands from November to
May. They migrate north for
the summer, to Maine and
beyond.

JOEL PETERSON

Stillness

Tarpaulin Cove, Naushon. John Murray Forbes of Milton, Massachusetts, became the owner of Naushon Island when he married the previous owner's niece in 1854. Forbes died in 1898, leaving the island in the Forbes Family Trust in perpetuity. At last count, he had some 300 living descendants.

GAYLE HEASLIP

Implements

View from the wood shop on Penikese Island. In 1973 George Cadwalader established a school on Penikese for delinquent boys in the custody of the state Department of Youth Services. The boys of Penikese take classes, work with wood, grow their own vegetables and do without electricity or running water.

ABOVE

ABOVE

JOEL PETERSON

Reflecting Pool

Land view of Tarpaulin Cove,
Naushon. During the
Revolution, a hundred sailors
off the British sloop Faulkland
came ashore here and made
off with all the livestock they
could carry. Later, they built a
barracks not far from this
spot. It was here, too, that the
British brig Nimrod anchored
in 1814, before and after her
three-hour bombardment of
Falmouth.

OPPOSITE

JOEL PETERSON

Marine Railway

Hadley's Harbor, Naushon.
Hadley's is a secure and lovely
little harbor open to any boat
that wishes to shelter there,
thanks to the Forbes family,
who own Naushon in trust.

JOEL PETERSON

Strollers

The beach at Tarpaulin Cove,
Naushon. The farmhouse is
one of several summer island
residences of the Forbes family,
who own Naushon through the
Forbes Family Trust. The public
is welcome to come ashore.

ACKNOWLEDGEMENTS

The publishers would like to acknowledge many
people who helped with this book.

To Joel and Sue Peterson for their advice and enthusiasm.

Thanks to John Hough, Jr. for the captions. Mr. Hough is a columnist
for *The Falmouth Enterprise* and the author of three novels, including
The Conduct of the Game. As he grew up in Falmouth and a lifelong
resident of the Upper Cape, his detailed knowledge of the area as well as
his enthusiasm significantly expanded upon the images that we present
here. Mr. Hough now makes his home on Martha's Vineyard.

And to Brenda Swithenbank for continued
suggestions, support and encouragement.